The Never-Told Story

The train slowly chugged along.
Betsy was tired of riding
and riding.

"Please tell me a story, Dad,"
she said.

Dad thought and thought.
Betsy waited and waited.

"Did I tell you the story
of the big, bad wolf?"
Dad asked.

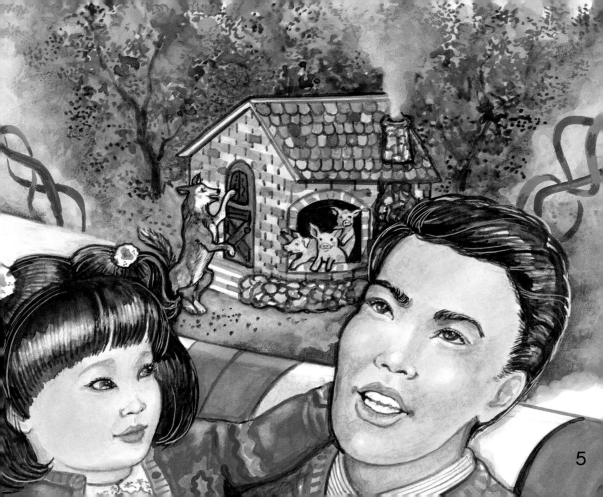

5

"Yes, about ten times,"
Betsy said.
"Tell me a new story, please."

6

Dad thought and thought.
Betsy waited and waited.

"Did I tell you the story
of the princess and the frog?"
Dad asked.

"Yes, about twenty times,"
Betsy said.
"Tell me a new story, please."

Dad thought and thought.
Betsy waited and waited.

"Did I tell you the story
of the giant and his herd
of grumpy pigs?" Dad asked.

13

"No! I have NEVER heard that story!" Betsy said. "Please tell me that one."

14

"Once upon a time..." Dad said.
"Hey, wait a minute – we're here!"